THE
HOME
YOU MADE
~ for ME ~

CELEBRATING A
Mother's Love

THOMAS KINKADE *Painter of Light*™

Publishers Since 1798

THOMAS NELSON PUBLISHERS®
Nashville

The Home You Made for Me

Published in Nashville, Tennessee, by Thomas Nelson, Inc.

Design and production by: Quebecor World Digital Services, Chicago

ISBN 0-7852-6962-2

Printed in the United States of America
2 3 4 5 6 7 QPK 05 04 03 02 01 00

Presented to:

Linda Rogers Baldiga — my beautiful mother —

On this ___12th___ day

of ___May, 2002___

By ___Lisa___

With this special message:

Mom, I just want you to know how grateful I am for you, and all your love + support over the years. You truly are a great "Mom" in every sense of the word. I love you

Mother

The older we grow the more precious become the recollections
of our childhood days, especially our memories of mother.
Her love and care halo her memory with brighter
radiance, for we have discovered that nowhere else in
the world is such loving self-sacrifice to be found;
her counsels and instructions appeal to us with greater
force than when we received them because our
knowledge of the world and our experience
of life have proved their worth.

Dearer even than mother's
teachings are little, personal
memories of her, different
in each case but essentially
the same—mother's face,
mother's touch, mother's voice:

Childhood's days were full of joy,

So merry bright and gay;

On sunny wings of happiness

Swiftly they flew away.

But oh! By far the sweetest hour

Of all the whole day long

Was the slumber hour at twilight

And my mother's voice in song—

"Hush, my babe; be still and slumber,

Holy Angels guard thy bed,

Heavenly blessings without number

Gently resting on thy head."

Though our days are filled with gladness,

Joys of lifelike sunshine fall;

Still life's slumber hour at twilight

May be sweetest of them all.

And when to the realms of boundless peace,

I am waiting to depart

Then my mother's song at twilight

Will make music in my heart.

"Hush, my babe, lie still and slumber;

Holy angels guard thy bed."

And I'll fall asleep so sweetly,

Mother's blessings on my head.

–LAURA INGALLS WILDER, SEPTEMBER 1921

A family's love makes a house a home.

–Thomas Kinkade

❧

Mothers… fill places so great that there
isn't an angel in heaven who wouldn't be
glad to give a bushel of diamonds to come
down and take their place.

–Billy Sunday

❧

How beautifully everything
is arranged by Nature;
as soon as a child enters
the world, it finds a mother
ready to take care of it.

–Jules Michelet

All that I am my mother made me.

–John Quincy Adams

✃

The best occupation on the earth for a
woman is to be a real mother to her
children. It does not have much glory in it;
there is a lot of grit and grime. But there is
no greater place of ministry, position, or
power than that of a mother.

–Phil Whisenhunt

✃

My mother had a great deal of trouble
with me, but I think she enjoyed it.

–Mark Twain

One of my happiest memories of you is...

❧

... how through all the different times between Dad & I, you always tried to cover for me, to be on my team as best you could. It couldn't have been easy on you to be in that position, but I felt your love for me even though you were in a terrible position.

By wisdom a house is built,

and through understanding it is established;

through knowledge its rooms are filled

with rare and beautiful treasures.

– PROVERBS 24:3–4 (NIV)

The kingdom of home as well as the

Kingdom of Heaven is within.

–LAURA INGALLS WILDER

Babies are such a nice way

to start people.

–DON HAROLD

To My Mother

You too, my mother, read my rhymes

For love of unforgotten times,

And you may chance to hear once more

The little feet along the floor.

–ROBERT LOUIS STEVENSON

❧

I am beginning to learn that it is the sweet,

simple things of life which are the real

ones after all.

–LAURA INGALLS WILDER

Sutter Creek
Inn
BIG1 #

WELCOME

Reading a message from my mother, I am a child again and a longing unutterable fills my heart for Mother's counsel, for the safe haven of her protection and the relief from responsibility which trusting in her judgment always gave me.

–LAURA INGALLS WILDER

&

Never trust anyone with a secret—except your mother.

–IRENE ZAHAVA

&

A baby is an angel whose wings decrease as his legs increase.

–FRENCH PROVERB

God Gave to Me a Child in Part

God gave to me a child in part,

Yet wholly gave the father's heart:

Child of my soul, O whither now,

Unborn, unmothered, goest thou?

You came, you went, and no man wist;

Hapless, my child, no breast you kist;

On no dear knees, a privileged babbler, clomb,

Nor knew the kindly feel of home.

My voice may reach you, O my dear-

A father's voice perhaps the child may hear;

And, pitying, you may turn your view

On that poor father whom you never knew.

Alas! alone he sits, who then,

Immortal among mortal men,

Sat hand in hand with love, and all day through

With your dear mother wondered over you.

–ROBERT LOUIS STEVENSON

A Personal Note....

❧

We share a bond that not many have, we made it through those difficult years of my drinking & the pain that Dad inflicted, not only on me, but on you & all of us as a family, and look at how far we've come,

I'm so glad you've found the love that you have with Lenny, it gives me hope...

Being a full-time mother is one of the highest salaried jobs in my field, since the payment is pure love.

–MILDRED B. VERMONT

❧

I believe the most stirring moment in the experience of a parent comes on the day he leaves the child in school for the first time. This can be so sharp an experience that, when there are two or three children, this ritual has to be alternated between parents.

–HARVEY GOLDEN

The illusions of childhood are necessary experiences. A child should not be denied a balloon because an adult knows that sooner or later it will burst.

–Marcelene Cox

Judicious mothers will always keep in mind that they are the first book read, and the last put aside, in every child's library.

–C. Lenox Reonond

Thomas Kinkade

The happiest moments of my life have
been the few which I have passed at home
in the bosom of my family.

  – THOMAS JEFFERSON

A house built of lasting materials would be
a much better monument to one's memory
than a costly stone in a cemetery.

  –LAURA INGALLS WILDER

Teaching kids to count is fine, but teaching
them what counts is best.

  –BOB TALBERT

A house is no home unless it contains food
and fire for the mind as well as for the body.

–Margaret Fuller

The wise woman builds her house,
But the foolish pulls it down with her hands.
He who walks in his uprightness fears
the LORD.

– Proverbs 14:1–2

Faith is a constant thread
strengthening the fabric of
our family.

–Thomas Kinkade

You made our home special because...

❧

You just always led with your heart, time after time when either Dave or I had done something once again, you never once shamed us, that truly is a blessing, even in your pain + disapointment you never have belittled us.

Thank you

THE HOME YOU MADE FOR ME

PYE CORNER
COTTAGE
WELCOME

Thomas
Kinkade

More than in any other human
relationship, overwhelmingly more,
motherhood means being instantly
interruptible, responsive, responsible.

–Tillie Olsen

Blessed be the childhood, which brings
down something of heaven into the midst
of our rough earthliness.

–Henri Frederic Ameil

Home is the place that'll catch you when
you fall. And we all fall.

– Billie Letts

God could not be everywhere so he created mothers.

–ANONYMOUS

Just as a little thread of gold, running through a fabric, brightens the whole garment, so women's work at home, while only the doing of little things, is just like the golden gleam of sunlight that runs through and brightens the whole fabric of civilization.

–LAURA INGALLS WILDER

Fill your home with love and laughter.

–THOMAS KINKADE

Out in the meadow, I picked a wild
sunflower, and, as I looked into its golden
heart, such a wave of homesickness came
over me that I almost wept…. Across the
years, the old home and its love called
to me, and memories of sweet words of
counsel came flooding back.

–LAURA INGALLS WILDER

Kind words can be short and easy to speak,
but their echoes are truly endless.

–MOTHER TERESA

Your family is a gift you have been given.

–THOMAS KINKADE

The laughter of a child is the light of a house.

–AFRICAN PROVERB

❧

By and large, mothers and housewives are the
only workers who do not have regular times off.
They are the great vacationless class.

–ANNE MORROW LINDBERGH

❧

If we, as mothers, are doing
a good job, we soon do
ourselves out of a job.

–KAREN SUMMAR HODGE

Special memories of our times together....

I always remember you patiently taking me school shopping. I bet that wasn't easy those years that I was heavy & sad & hated everything. You never once made me feel like you saw me as anything but perfect.

Again, thank you.

Parents learn a lot from their children about coping with life.

–MURIEL SPARK

My father would have enjoyed what you have so generously said of me and my mother would have believed every word of it.

–LYNDON B. JOHNSON

Rituals encase memories. They link the past and the present. They choreograph the dance of intimacy that families and friends perform. They give us access to one another.

–WENDY M. WRIGHT

I love little children, and it is not a slight thing when they, who are fresh from God, love us.

–Charles Dickens

Every person needs recognition. It is expressed cogently by the child who says, "Mother, let's play darts. I'll throw the darts and you say 'wonderful.'"

–M. Dale Baugham

Mama, as always, was prepared for the unexpected, and with her compassionate heart made each stranger feel a part of the family.

–Margaret Jensen

Thomas Kinkade

It is the mother who can cure
her child's fears.

–AFRICAN PROVERB

There's a time when you have to
explain to your children the reason
why they're born, and it's a marvelous
thing if you know the reason by then.

–HAZEL SCOTT

A mother who is really a
mother is never free.

–HONORÉ DE BALZAC

Maternal love. A substance which
God multiplies as he divides it.

–Victor Hugo

For most of us the mention of family
brings back fond memories of a distant
past—of times so good they overshadow
the difficulties. Home is the place where
we can go when we're tired and lonely;
it is here in the family that we can be
ourselves and still know we are accepted.

–Author Unknown

Children's talent to endure stems from
their ignorance of alternatives.

–Maya Angelou

One of my happiest memories of you is...

❧

Believe it or not, all the times that you came to visit me in my various hospital stays, I was so scared + I must have broken your heart to see me in those places, but you were always there with words of encouragement + your time - you've always made time for us kids when we really need you

Thank you

THE HOME YOU MADE FOR ME

Just as you inherit your mother's brown eyes,

you inherit part of yourself.

–Alice Walker

If what has hitherto been woman's work in the
world is simply left undone by them, there is no one
else to take it up. If ... their old and special work
is neglected and only half done, there will be
something seriously wrong with the world, for the
commonplace home work of women is the very
foundation upon which everything else rests.

–Laura Ingalls Wilder

By giving children lots of affection, you can
help fill them with love and acceptance of
themselves. Then that's what they will have
to give away.

–Dr. Wayne Dyer

Honor your father and your mother,
that your days may be long upon the land
which the LORD your God is giving you.

–Exodus 20:12

A mother's arms are made of tenderness
and children sleep soundly in them.

–Victor Hugo

Such magic there is in Christmas to draw the
absent ones home, and, if unable to go in the body,
the thoughts will hover there! Our hearts grow tender
with childhood memories and love of kindred, and
we are better throughout the year for having, in spirit,
become a child again at Christmastime.

–Laura Ingalls Wilder

Good works are links that form a chain of love.

–Mother Teresa

CHRISTMAS
OPEN
HOUSES

The mother is the medium through which
the primitive infant transforms himself into
a socialized human being.

–BEATON RANK

A family is a place where principles are
hammered and honed on the anvil of
everyday living.

–CHARLES SWINDOLL

If the members of a home are ill-tempered
and quarrelsome, how quickly you feel it
when you enter the house. You may not
know what is wrong, but you wish to make
your visit short.

–LAURA INGALLS WILDER

Thank you for making the holidays so special. Some of my favorite family traditions are...

... how you always filled the stockings & left them outside our bedroom door, and insisted on going downstairs first to turn on the tree lights

... how the house was decorated for every holiday

THE HOME YOU MADE FOR ME

61

Is not a young mother one of the sweetest
sights which life shows us?

–WILLIAM THACKERAY

My son, keep your father's command,

And do not forsake the law of your mother.

Bind them continually upon your heart;

Tie them around your neck.

When you roam, they will lead you;

When you sleep, they will keep you;

And when you awake, they will speak

with you.

–PROVERBS 6: 20–22

There are three ways to get something done;

do it yourself, hire someone, or forbid your kids to do it.

–Michel de Montaigne

They say that man is mighty,

He governs land and sea,

He wields a mighty scepter

O'er lesser powers than he.

But a mighty power and stronger

Man from his throne has hurled;

For the hand that rocks the cradle

Is the hand that rules the world.

–William Wallace

A baby is God's opinion that

the world should go on.

–Carl Sandburg

To make your children capable of honesty
is the beginning of education.

–JOHN RUSKIN

Being constantly with children is like
wearing a pair of shoes that were expensive
and too small. She couldn't bear to throw
them out, but they gave her blisters.

–BERYL BAINBRIDGE

No matter how old a mother is she
watches her middle-aged children for
signs of improvement.

–FLORA SCOTT MAXWELL

We find delight in the beauty and
happiness of children that makes the
heart too big for the body.

–Ralph Waldo Emerson

Just about the time she thinks her work
is done, a mother becomes a grandmother.

–Anonymous

If evolution really works, how come
mothers still only have two hands?

–Ed Dussault

Thomas
Kinkade

A Personal Note....

❧

I'm so glad that God
gave me you as a
mother. You truly have been
a blessing in my
life

Not only was Monday wash day, it was also soup day. The scraps dropped into the kettle of homemade soup and the loaves of Mama's rye bread seemed to multiply like the loaves and fishes in the New Testament story. Regardless of the number of unexpected guests, there was always enough. God and Mama could do anything!

–MARGARET JENSEN

My joy burns brighter when I tend to the glowing hearth fires of home.

–THOMAS KINKADE

Thomas Kinkade

The mother should teach her daughter
above all things to know herself.

–C. E. SARGENT

What do you think of when you hear the
word home? What images and emotions
come to mind? This is something to
ponder, for these images and emotions
have the power to shape your life, to give
it meaning, to tell you who you are.

–THOMAS KINKADE

What do you do with mother love
and mother when babies are grown
and gone away?

–JOANNE GREENBERG

A hundred years from now it will not matter
what my bank account was, the sort of house
I lived in, or the kind of car I drove.
But the world may be different because
I was important in the life of a child.

–AUTHOR UNKNOWN

Lessons learned at mother's knee last
through life.

–LAURA INGALLS WILDER

There are two things in life for which we are
never fully prepared, and that is–twins.

–JOSH BILLINGS

'Tis the gift to be simple, 'tis the gift to be free,

'Tis the gift to come down where we ought to be,

And when we find ourselves in the place just right,

'Twill be in the valley of love and delight.

–Traditional Shaker Hymn

Train your Child in the way in which you should

have gone yourself.

–Charles H. Spurgeon

I begin to love this little creature, and to anticipate

his birth as a fresh twist to a knot, which I do not

want to untie.

–Mary Wollstonecraft

*S*pecial memories of
our times together...

❧

Blackberry picking up behind
Grampy + Grammies + you telling
me the story of how you broke
your leg on a big rock or piece of
concrete or something, up there by
the old truck, remember...?

THE HOME YOU MADE FOR ME

Oh, what a power is motherhood, possessing a potent spell. All women alike fight fiercely for a child.

—Euripides

⚬

If a woman remains unmarried, is appointed matron of an orphanage and brings up other people's children to be good Christians, she is called a church worker. But if she marries, becomes the mother of a family and brings up her children to be good Christians, no one calls her a church worker, yet that good mother is a church worker.

—Billy Sunday

Children should be led into the right paths,
not by severity, but by persuasion.

–Terence

What is there in the attitude of your children
toward yourself that you wish were different?
Search your own heart and learn if your ways
toward your own mother could be improved.

–Laura Ingalls Wilder

Mother is far too clever to understand
anything she does not like.

–Arnold Bennett

I looked on child rearing not only as a work of love and duty but as a profession . . . that demanded the best that I could bring to it.

–Rose Kennedy

Instant availability without continuous presence is probably the best role a mother can play.

–Lotte Bailyn

When I think back to my own childhood days, the words that seem to fill my memories and epitomize my childhood are: "Let's do it." I'm convinced there's something in that "let's do it now" mentality that is a vital secret to childlike joy. There's something inherently joyous about being able to think of something great to do and then jump into the idea with both bare feet.

–Thomas Kinkade

Pretty much all the honest truth telling there is in the world is done by children.

–Oliver Wendell Holmes

❧

My son, hear the instruction of your father,
And do not forsake the law of your mother;
For they will be a graceful ornament on your head,
And chains about your neck.

–Proverbs 1:8–9

These are some of the things you taught me that I hope to pass on to my children.

If I was to ever have children the biggest thing that you have taught me that I would hope to pass on is unconditional love, that love holds firm in the face of disappointment...

She never quite leaves her children at home,

even when she doesn't take them along.

–Charles H. Spurgeon

Listen to your father who begot you,

And do not despise your mother when she is old.

Buy the truth, and do not sell it,

Also wisdom and instruction and understanding.

The father of the righteous will greatly rejoice,

And he who begets a wise child will delight in him.

Let your father and your mother be glad,

And let her who bore you rejoice.

–Proverbs 23:22–25

How many hope and fears, how many ardent wishes
and anxious apprehensions are twisted together in the
threads that connect the parent with the child!

–Samuel Griswold Goodrich

Where parents do too much for their children,
their children do too little for themselves.

–Elbert Hubbard

Parents must get across the idea that "I love you always,
but sometimes I do not love your behavior."

–Amy Vanderbilt

One knows one's done one's job as a
parent properly if one's children reject
everything one stands for.

–Glenda Jackson

Children aren't happy with nothing
to ignore. And that's what parents
were created for.

–Ogden Nash

A truly appreciative child will break,
lose, spoil, or fondle to death any really
successful gift within a matter of minutes.

–Russell Lyons

A Personal Note....

❧

I'm glad that we have gone a different path than the one shown to you by your mom. I suppose this may be painful for you, but although your mom was + has always been distant + vague with her love, you have dared to reach out with your heart + love me + be there for me in a way that she has never been able to do for you. that is so huge. Thank you for daring to love, really love.

Again, Thank you

God pardons like a mother who kisses the
offense into everlasting forgetfulness.

–HENRY WARD BEECHER

❧

Mama's abounding joy of living carried our
family and congregation through many crises.
We learned that the joy of the Lord was our
strength. Proverbs 15:15 belonged to Mama:
"He that is of a merry heart
hath a continual feast."

– MARGARET JENSEN

A man loves his sweetheart the most, his wife the best,

but his mother the longest.

–Irish proverb

Nature

As a fond mother, when the day is o'er,

Leads by the hand her little child to bed,

Half willing, half reluctant to be led

And leave his broken playthings on the floor.

Still gazing at them through the open door,

Nor wholly reassured and comforted

By promises of other sin their stead,

Which, though more splendid, may not please him more;

So Nature deals with us, and takes away

Our playthings one by one, and by the hand

Leads us to rest so gently, that we go

Scarce knowing if we wish to go or stay.

Being too full of sleep to understand

How far the unknown transcends the what we know.

–Henry Wadsorth Longfellow

A girl is Innocence playing in the mud,

Beauty standing on its head, and

Motherhood dragging a doll by the foot.

–ALLEN BECK

In case you are worried about what is going

to become of the younger generation,

it's going to grow up and start worrying

about the younger generation.

–ROGER ALLEN

A woman who can cope with the terrible

twos can cope with anything.

–JUDITH CLABES

Special memories of our times together...

✦

I'll always bee grateful
for our trip to New York, all
the generations + on your 50th Birthday,
and who ever could have known what
would have become of the twin towers.

To the mother of young children, there is a
time and place for everything, except rest.

–Anonymous

⚘

Train up a child in the way he should go,
And when he is old he will not depart from it.

–Proverbs 22:6

⚘

Her children rise up and call her blessed.

–Proverbs 31:28 (NKJV)

Who takes the child by the hand
takes the mother by the heart.

–Danish Proverb

❧

Children hold spring so tightly in their
brown fists—just as grown-ups, who are less
sure of it, hold it in their hearts.

–E. B. White

At noon, Mama always stopped for lunch and nap time. No one—on any day—escaped the nap. Papa went quietly to his study. The house grew still. The children slept. Mama rested thirty minutes (surely she didn't sleep), then rose quietly. She brushed out her long brown hair and put on a crisp starched dress and apron. To complete her preparations for the second half of her day, she sat down and opened her Bible. After reading she quietly slipped to her knees for her afternoon talk with God. Mama's prayer time was as sure as the sun coming up in the morning. Even the youngest child knew to be quiet until Mama was finished.

–MARGARET JENSEN

Sutter Creek Inn

WELCOME

Thomas
Kinkade

Thank you for your Godly example.
I hope to be more like you in these ways:

Your quiet grace, your constant thoughtfulness, your undeniable courage to face difficult situations with love + patience, your ability to change. I've always admired you for leaving a man who made you unhappy, even though 19 years held you together. You dared follow your heart + invite a truer love into your life.

THE HOME YOU MADE FOR ME

The Mother's Hymn

Lord, who ordainest for mankind
Benignant toils and tender cares,
We thank Thee for the ties that bind
The mother to the child she bears.

We thank Thee for the hopes that rise
Within her heart as day by day,
The dawning soul, from these young eyes,
Looks with a clearer, steadier ray.

And grateful for the blessing given
With that dear infant on her knee,
She trains the eye to look to heaven,
The voice to lisp a prayer to Thee.

Such thanks the blessed Mary gave
When from her lap the Holy Child,
Sent from on high to seek and to save
The lost of earth, looked up and smiled.

All-Gracious! Grant to those who bear
A mother's charge the strength and light
To guide the feet that own their care
In ways of love and truth and right.

—William Cullen Bryant

To Any Reader

As from the house your mother sees

You playing round the garden trees,

So you may see, if you but look

Another child, far, far away,

And in another garden, play.

But do not think you can at all,

by knocking on the window, call

That child to hear you. He intent

Is still on his play-business bent.

He does not hear; he will not look,

Nor yet be lured out of this book.

For long ago, the truth to say,

He has grown up and gone away,

And it is but a child of air

That lingers in the garden there.

–Robert Louis Stevenson

An ounce of mother is worth a pound of clergy.

–SPANISH PROVERB

⚬

Of all the joys that lighten suffering on earth,
what joy is welcomed like that of a newborn child.

–CAROLINE NORTON

⚬

Every baby born into
the world is a finer one
than the last.

–CHARLES DICKENS

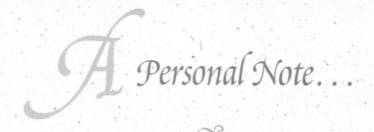

A Personal Note....

I can only hope that I
can make you as proud to have
me as a daughter, as I am to
have you as a mother.

For it is the security that comes from truly being at home that gives one the courage and freedom to travel, to seek adventure. And it is the warmth and connection of home that gives meaning to the time I spend away.

–THOMAS KINKADE

Home is Heaven for beginners.

– CHARLES PARKHURST

My mother was the source from which I
derived the guiding principles of my life.

–John Wesley

Much is being said of the present crisis in
the world and the need to do something
about it. But to play a part and do our duty,
we do not need to be the principal actors.
We have only to be good citizens, good
neighbor and – most of all – good parents.

–Lucious D. Clay

Mother Passed Away

"Mother passed away this morning" was the message that came over the wires, and a darkness overshadowed the spring sunshine; a sadness crept into the bird's songs.

Some of us have received such messages. Those who have not, one day will. Just as when a child, home was lonely when mother was gone, so to children of a larger growth, the world becomes a lonesome place when mother has passed away and only memories of her are left us—happy memories if we have not given ourselves any cause for regret.

Memories! We go through life collecting them whether we will or not! Sometimes I wonder if they are our treasures in Heaven or the consuming fires of torment when we carry them with us as we, too, pass on.

What a joy our memories may be or what a sorrow! But glad or sad they are with us forever. Let us make them carefully of all good things, rejoicing in the wonderful truth that while we are laying up for ourselves the very sweetest and best of happy memories, we are at the same time giving them to others.

–LAURA INGALLS WILDER,
WRITTEN UPON THE DEATH OF HER MOTHER,
CAROLINE QUINTER INGALLS, JUNE 1924